Inside an
Ant Colony

By Allan Fowler

Consultants
Linda Cornwell, Learning Resource Consultant,
Indiana Department of Education

S̶̶ ̶̶F̶̶ ̶̶ Elementary Science/Math Specialist,

JOHNSON SCHOOL ta
LLC

P Children's Press®
A Division of Grolier Publishing
New York   London   Hong Kong   Sydney
Danbury, Connecticut

Visit Children's Press® on the Internet at:
http://publishing.grolier.com

Designer: Herman Adler Design Group

Library of Congress Cataloging-in-Publication Data

Fowler, Allan.
    Inside an ant colony / by Allan Fowler.
      p. cm. — (Rookie read-about science)
    Includes index.
    Summary: Describes how these social insects live and work together in organized communities that are like bustling cities.
    ISBN 0-516-20804-7 (lib. bdg.)   0-516-26365-X (pbk.)
    1. Ants—Juvenile literature. 2. Insect societies—Juvenile literature.
[1. Ants.] I. Title. II. Series.
QL568.F7F64   1998   97-23300
595.79'6—dc21   CIP
                                         AC

Ants always seem to be busy.
You often see them hurry out
of a hole in the ground . . .

. . . or scurry back into it.

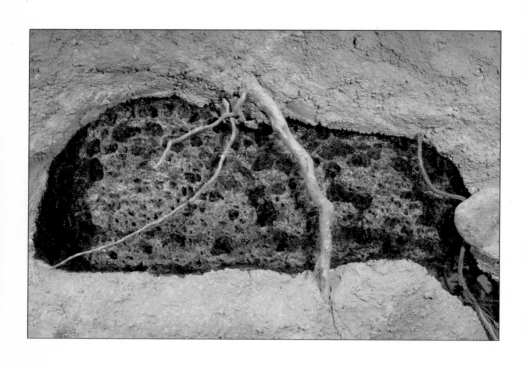

That hole is the entrance
to an ant colony. Each
ant colony is like an
underground city.

It has rooms, called chambers, where the ants live and work. Tunnels connect the chambers.

Some kinds of ants build hills around the entrances to their colonies.

They make the hills out of
soil and twigs.

Not all ants nest underground.
Carpenter ants live in trees,
or in dead wood, or in the
wooden walls of buildings.

Some ants build hills as high as the ceiling of your classroom.

Some colonies are very
small, with just a few ants.

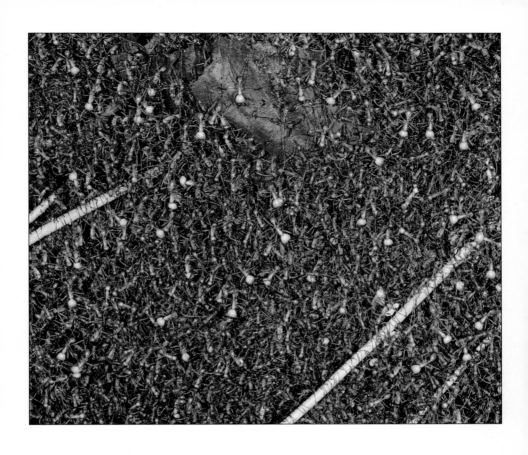

A big colony could have
as many ants as a big city
has people.

Just like people in a city, ants work at many different jobs.

Most of the ants in a colony are workers.

The workers are females that have no wings and cannot lay eggs.

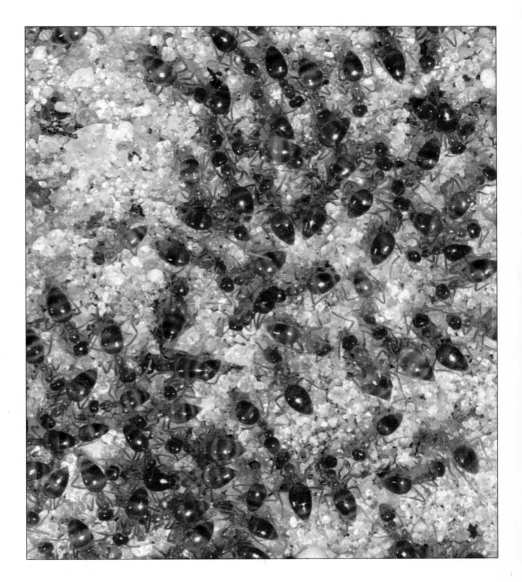

Some workers look after
the youngest ants.

Some gather food and bring
it to a storage chamber.

Other worker ants dig out
tunnels, or build ant hills,
or keep the colony clean.

The colony might have a chamber where the ants keep insects called aphids, the way human farmers keep cows. Ants "milk" aphids for a sweet liquid that they drink.

Queen ants have wings
and are much larger than
the workers.

A queen lives in her own chamber, where the workers look after her. A colony may have one queen, or many.

Male ants also have wings. In summer, a new queen flies away with the males to mate. Then she sheds her wings and starts a new colony, or returns to her old one.

The queen stays in the colony for the rest of her life, laying eggs. Queens often live 15 to 20 years.

Only a queen can lay eggs.
Larvae hatch from the eggs
and become new ants.

There are thousands of
different kinds of ants.
Fire ants can sting.

Army ants travel across the land, like a huge army, eating almost every small animal in their path.

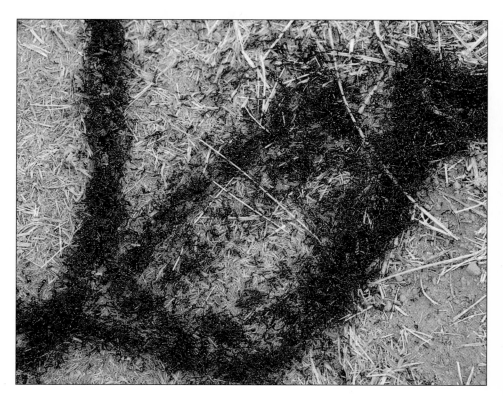

The biggest ants are
more than an inch long.

Others are so small that several of them could fit inside the hole in the letter "a" of "ants."

Big or small, an ant is strong. It can lift things much heavier than its own body.

Have you ever seen a tiny leaf-cutter ant carrying a big piece of a leaf over its head?

One way to learn what happens in an ant colony is to study an ant farm. A whole colony of ants lives inside a clear plastic or glass box.

The ants work so hard that
just watching them might
make you tired!

Words You Know

ant farm

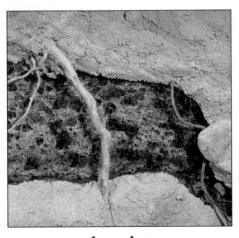

chamber

tunnels

aphids

workers

queen ant

eggs

larvae

army ants

carpenter ants

fire ant

leaf-cutter ant

31

Index

About the Author

Allan Fowler is a freelance writer with a background in advertising. Born in New York, he now lives in Chicago and enjoys traveling.

Photo Credits

©: Animals Animals: 9 (A. Ecker), 4, 30 bottom left (Zig Leszczynski), 7, 14, 20, 31 middle left (Raymond A. Mendez); Bruce Coleman: 28 (Bob Gossington); Comstock: 3 (Townsend P. Dickinson), 5, 25, 30 bottom right; Doug Wechsler: cover; Ellis Nature Photography: 27, 31 bottom right (Gerry Ellis); Photo Researchers: 8, 31 bottom left (Ted Clutter), 11, 16, 23, 31 middle right (Gregory G. Dimijian), 17, 31 top left (Michael McCoy), 6 (Kathy Merrifield), 22, 31 bottom center (J.H. Robinson), 15 (Dr. Frieder Sauer/OKAPIA), 21, 31 middle center (Kenneth H. Thomas), 24 (Paul A. Zahl); Stephen Feld: 29, 30 top; Unicorn Stock Photos: 10 (Tommy Dodson); Wildlife Collection: 13, 31 top center (Clay Myers), 18, 31 top right (Bob Parks).